YOU
HAVE BEEN
CHOSEN!

YOU
HAVE BEEN
CHOSEN!
REJECTED BY MAN BUT CHOSEN BY GOD

JOANN LACEY SANTIAGO

Library of Congress Control Number: 2019917540
ISBN: Hardcover   978-1-7960-6900-6
                 Softcover   978-1-7960-6899-3
                 eBook   978-1-7960-6898-6

Print information available on the last page.

Rev. date: 10/30/2019

To order additional copies of this book, contact:
Xlibris
1-888-795-4274
www.Xlibris.com
Orders@Xlibris.com
798018

TABLE OF CONTENTS

ABOUT THE AUTHOR

Dr. Santiago was born in NJ attended the public schools and graduated from Caldwell College with her B.A. in Sociology, a minor in Psychology and certificate in Criminal Justice Studies. Dr. Santiago is also a graduate of Lighthouse Christian College with her Master degree in Theology and Ph.D. in Religious Education. She has been licensed to teach all levels of ministry by ETA.

She has worked and volunteered in many social services, and has worked in the Emergency room of the local hospital and in different government positions. She believes in helping others naturally and spiritually.

Dr. Santiago has been writing since the age of 10 and has had some of her poetic writings published in a number of books. She was published in a Christian magazine which reached out to the African communities in NJ. She is the author of the book "The Prophetic Office of the Seer".

Apostle Santiago enjoys writing and teaching the Word of God. She has taught at biblical and prophetic schools. Apostle JoAnn Lacey Santiago is called by God as his Seer prophet and was affirmed as an Apostle of the Lord Jesus Christ in 2010. Her desire is to do the will of Lord and teach his word according to Ephesians 4:13.

> *"Till we all come in the unity of the faith and of the knowledge of the son of God, unto a perfect man, unto the measure of the stature of the fullness of Christ"*

DEDICATION

I would like to dedicate this book in loving memory to my Aunt Mattie Sykes and Mother Connie Simmons who prayed for me.

You are always in my heart.

I also would like to give special thanks to my parents Tazewell and Joyce Lacey and my husband Antonio. Thank you for your heartfelt support and guidance.

Also to Apostle Dorothy and Deacon William Matthews and the Word of Power church family, thank you for your love, care, support and prayers. May the Lord bless each of you with your heart's desire according to his will.

Most of all I thank God for all my experiences that has trained, taught, rebuked, kept, encouraged, grew, chastised and continue to stretch me. If it had not been for God who was one my side; where would I be? Thank you Jesus for saving me!

Despite it all, I have been chosen and if you have picked up this book so have you.

Remember many are called but few are chosen.

God bless you!

You have been CHOSEN!

PREFACE

Many times you may feel like you have been chosen, to do a specific job or to deliver a specific message; even to say a specific thing to a specific people. Often you know your assignment, and it seems so very clear, but there are times you are rejected by others and then feel unable to fulfill that thing you long to do.

I am not talking about those who want a special place and are not equipped or even called to it. I am talking about those who know who they are and what they are here to do.

Just because someone says no, or you cannot, or not you, does not mean you should give up on your assignment. When God calls you he equips you and he sends you, not man. Doors may close but doors will open if you just let patience have her perfect work.

God has a way of bringing everything to completeness even if you think it may end another way. Trust God, he knows exactly what he is doing. It may look stagnated, held up, or held back but there is a divine set time for you and your assignment.

I hope this book will encourage you to not just linger around being a called out one, but to advance and do what you and only you have been chosen to do.

I will address a few characters of the bible and how they were rejected by men but chosen by God for their particular area of work. We are not better than our Lord who himself came unto his own and was not received. He was able to complete his assignment through rejection, hurt and pain.

Jesus was chosen by God. Rejection did not stop Him, and he did not quit. My hope is that you will be encouraged and not quit. You may feel rejected by man but you must push through knowing that you have been accepted and chosen by God.

You are needed, and wanted, and loved.

You have been CHOSEN for such a time as this!

INTRODUCTION

Let us first get the definition of the words reject and chosen. According to the Webster Dictionary to reject is to:

1. To refuse to accept or to make use of
2. To refuse to recognize or consider
3. To discard as defective or useless
4. To throw away
5. To disallow or disesteem
6. To break faith with or to cast away

At some point in this life you will experience some form of rejection. We all have, and it does not feel good. There may be a time when you will look back at the situation and see some good it produced. It does not have to be all bad. Glean the good and learn.

There is still some growing that has to take place. There even may be some humbling that has to happen before you are fully released to accomplish what the Father has ordained for you to do. It is called the process.

Go through the process and learn all you can. Keep standing and by all means; keep praying. You will come through intact, without bitterness, or retaliation. You must walk in forgiveness and always remember to love.

According to Webster to be chosen is:

1. to be selected from
2. to be one of the elect
3. a choosing for a particular purpose that causes one to respond to God's election.

When you are chosen there is a response due from you. God is waiting for you to step up and step out. There is no trouble he cannot bring you out of, and no rejection he cannot cover with his love. You have to keep your focus on God and his assignment for you. If you look to man for deliverance or approval he may fail you. God will prepare you to be able to stand in any storm.

We all must give an account for the choices we make. God chooses whom he will for a particular work. He will equip you for it. Now it is up to you to choose to go where he has sent you, and do what he has said do.

Let us consider the life of a few characters of the bible. You will discover:

1. that it is God that chooses you to a particular work
2. it is he alone who will give you the instructions
3. your faith will be tried
4. proof that you can stand in the midst of persecution or rejection
5. that your pain has a purpose
6. and that joy will come in the morning.

God have called you. God made covenant with you. God equipped you and gave you His grace. So, understand that times may change, and people may change, but God will never leave you or forsake you. Trust him and he will give you the answers you are looking for.

Get ready,

YOU have been CHOSEN!

> *JOHN 1:1-11*
> *"In the beginning was the Word and the Word was with God and the Word was God. The same was in the beginning with God. All things were made by Him; and without Him was not anything made that was made. In Him was life. And the life was the light of men. And the Light shineth in darkness and the darkness comprehended it not. There was a man sent from God whose name was John. The same came for a witness, to bear witness of the Light that all men through Him might believe. He was not that Light, but was sent to bear witness of the Light. That was the true Light, which lighteth every man that cometh into the world. He was in the world, and the world was made by Him, and the world knew Him not.*

He came unto his own and His own received Him not."

A Chosen Reject

CHAPTER 1
Abraham

Genesis 12:1-4
"Now the Lord had said unto Abram, Get thee out of the country, and from thy kindred, and from thy father's house, unto a land that I will show thee:

And I will make of thee a great nation, and I will bless thee, and make thy name great; and thou shalt be a blessing:

And I will bless them that bless thee, and curse them that curseth thee: and in thee shall all families of the earth be blessed."

Abraham was called by God to leave his people and home for an unknown land. When God has called you, you will know his voice. He will prepare and send you. Abraham knew the voice of the Lord and understood what he was being asked to do. He had to make a response.

When God calls you out, your faith is put on trial. Will you answer the call? Will you choose to follow the leading of the Lord? Will you trust God and go despite what your family and friends may say? So many questions will come to your mind. Fear will try to get you to back away. Did Abraham have some fear or reservation? What would you do, and how would you respond if this was you?

It is beautiful to hear God promise Abraham something that no man could ever have offered him. God himself was going to bless Abraham. God himself was going to make Abraham's name great.

God was going to make Abraham a blessing to all the families of the earth. He is still a blessing even today. God was also his defense because he would curse those who would curse Abraham. This is how God will fight for you. He will repay and vengeance is his. Always remember that. You have to continue in love.

Abrahams' family may have thought that he was delusional or beside himself. They may have mocked him thinking he thought himself better than they. They may have even supported him, somewhat. Yet, he had to leave behind all that he knew. He left his culture, lifestyle, his family and friends. He went out by faith on a promise. He totally trusted God and left his comfort zone. He may have been ridiculed as he was packing to leave, but he never once retaliated. Rejection had come to take a front row seat but Abraham continued in love.

You may feel uncomfortable to step out into a place you are not familiar with. That is okay, your faith is being stretched. You need to know the voice of God so there is no doubt in what you are hearing. You must be able to first discern his voice, and wait for his instructions.

Abraham had to totally abandon his will to the will of God. He had made a choice. He responded to the call. He knew he was chosen. He wanted to follow after God. Being chosen you learn how to live in the place called never-the-less not my will but the will of the Lord be done. Abrahams' kindred may have felt he rejected them. Most do, when you step out by faith to do something that has never been done. He broke the family tradition.

Jesus broke the family traditions and his own family at one point, rejected him as well. It hurts; there is no doubt to that. When you expect those who love you to stand with you, and they leave you standing alone without support; it hurts. This is where you have to keep your head up and continue to look forward.

You may feel lonely and even look back as Abraham may have did hoping someone else was going to come along and yet see no one. Like Abraham keep moving. At some point you will forget the culture and traditions of your past and see all things in a new and godly way.

Abraham may have felt rejected. The only support was a nephew who wanted to go. We do not read of farewell parties or celebrations. He left and may have looked back as he went forward until he no longer could see where he had come from. Fear of not being able to see forward may even have gripped him from time to time. The voice of the Lord was yet leading him and would squash all that fear as he continued on.

If you feel fear, keep going forward it is only there to distract your mind and play in your imagination. Bring it into subjection to what God has said to you. There comes a time as you advance in your call that you begin to lose the fear of going forward and you realize that going back is no longer an option. You have come too far to retreat now. You begin to face a new day; every day in expectancy. Perfect love casts out all fear.

The longer you walk with God you will see your past differently. You will understand why some things turned out the way they did. You are learning from your past and looking forward to your future with a greater understanding.

When you accept the call, after you have been chosen, and you move forward; those things from your past begin to get smaller and smaller. You enter into the newness of Christ. You begin to press forward, expecting God to do just what he said he would do. You enter the place of expectation on a daily basis. Your faith and your hope are stronger and bigger. Do you expect the blessings of God daily? Yes! He promised new mercies every day.

Abraham was following the voice of a God that his family could not see or hear. They were used to their idol god statues made by man's hands who could not speak. They served gods made by man; when the true and living God made man with his hands, to serve Him. Who was this God of Abraham which they could not see with their own eyes nor feel with their own hands, they questioned?

At that time families had their own idol god that they would worship. Abraham was mature enough to make a decision of whom he would worship. God heard his heart as he searched for the true God. Abraham broke tradition.

How mature are you? Are you still following patterns set ages ago in your family that are not patterned after the true and living God. Think on that.

What God are you worshipping? God has a plan that has been set uniquely for you before the foundation of the world.

When you have been chosen by God you will not fit in the traditions of men. You will appear to them to be off or out of place; even a rebel. You may feel alone among a crowd of mockers. God will grace you with a breaker anointing to break out of the confines of mans' religious ideologies and into truth.

You will have a new way of thinking and believing. You will see the better way and your hope will be heavenly bound and unlimited. Turn and walk in the path that God has chosen for you and reap the promises of God. Pray for those who have not come to the place you are now at in God. Love them that have laughed and ridiculed you. Pray for them.

You can set a new atmosphere around you and sit in heavenly places in Christ Jesus. You are not confined to the earthly elements and restrictions. When you are chosen, your perception will change. You will see things from a different perspective; a higher level. You now see from Gods' perspective.

VERSES 4-5
"So Abram departed, as the Lord had spoken unto him; and Lot went with him: and Abram was seventy and five years old when he departed out of Haran.

*And Abram took Sarai his wife, and Lot his brother's son,
and all their substance that they had gathered, and the
souls that they had gotten in Haran; and they went forth
to go into the land of Canaan and into the land of Canaan
they came."*

We see instantly he gathered his belonging and his wife and
he was following his assignment. We also see there was a tag-
a-long that went with him. When God calls you and send you
out, you do not need anyone else hanging on your coat tail
riding off your blessing.

God will allow circumstances to separate them from you.
They can become weighty and cause a messy situation.
Abraham was sent and Lot just went. Tag-alongs can hinder
your blessing and slow down the work you are called to do. Be
wise about who is hanging on to you and why they are there.

You cannot take everyone with you. God chose you to bless
you and to provide for you. The anointing and blessing from
God was a costly price you paid. You suffered what you did
in preparation for the work.

Lot had nothing to lose. He was just going along to see what
this was all about and maybe get something out of it. Lot's
herd began to eat up what was provided for one set of herd,
namely Abrahams'.

Lot was drawing off the blessing of Abraham. He did not
pay the price of suffering through the ridicule, rejection and
mockery. He went for a free ride to the goodies, but God will
not allow his chosen to be taken advantage of. You will learn

this lesson if you are not careful and that tag-along will be cut loose.

The natural man is limited to what he can see and touch in the natural but with God there is no limit. Man may say you are useless for kingdom work and refuse to accept who you are. They may even reject you because you don't worship like they want you to or follow the protocols they have set.

God will accept you, recognize you as his choice and esteem you. When men discard you and throw you away, breaking faith with you; understand God will accept you, pick you up and make a covenant with you. God will bless you just like Abraham for your faithfulness. His promises are yea and amen.

Abraham may have been rejected by man but he was chosen by God. Use that rejection to push forward and work. Separate yourself from any weight that will try to hinder or bind you. God made a promise to you. You have been chosen.

CHOSEN TO RECEIVE THE PROMISES OF GOD!

CHAPTER 2

Noah

Genesis 6:5-8
"And God saw that the wickedness of man was great in the earth, and that every imagination of the thoughts of his heart was only evil continually.

And it repented the Lord that he had made man on the earth, and it grieved him at his heart.

And the Lord said, I will destroy man whom I have created from the face of the earth; both man, and beast, and the creeping thing, and the fowls of the air; for it repenteth me that I have made them.

But Noah found grace in the eyes of the Lord."

Noah had found favor with God. His grace was towards him. He had been chosen for a special project and there was no one else who was appointed for it. Like Noah, when God chooses you, he has a job that is designed just for you. He will grace you to complete the task. When God makes man a promise there is a response required from the one he has chosen. It was not anything according to the will of Noah or Abraham, but it was all according to the will of God.

When you try to merge your will with what God has willed to be, it can get a little dicey as we saw with Lot and Abraham. What state would the world be in if Noah had brought a tag along? We may think something or someone may be a help to us, but in reality it may just change the course of Gods' design and purpose.

In Genesis 6:9 it states: *"These are the generations of Noah: Noah was a just man and perfect in his generations, and Noah walked with God."*

In Noah's time wickedness was rampant on in the world, but his generations kept moving forward in God. They did not compromise, but stayed true to the word and will of God. In his lineage there was no mixing with the angels. They were perfect. The bible says he was just, and with justice there is also mercy.

His generations followed the pattern that God had ordained continually. They became perfected in what they did for God. They followed the plan that was given and salvation came.

The meaning of to save is to heal. If you follow the plan of God he will heal, save, deliver, and prosper you. You will receive the promise of God and others will be blessed. Will you do what he asks so you become a blessing for someone else? Abraham did and so did Noah.

Now the promise to Noah in Genesis 6:18 states,

> *"But with thee will I establish my covenant; and thou shalt come into the ark, thou and thy sons, and thy wife, and thy son's wives with thee; and they shall be male and female."*

God tells Noah I will save you and your household. Noah and his family received a pardon from the Lord by his grace.

With all that was going on in the world; God saw Noah. God is very particular about who he chooses. With all that stench of sin in the world, he still could smell a sweet odor of worship coming off Noah's generations.

If the rest of mankind in Noah's day had heeded the warning, the cry, and the call and repented they may have received a pardon too. Many were called but only a few were chosen.

It is because of the righteousness of the chosen that you and I have heard and accepted the call to come into the ark of safety in Christ Jesus. Jesus was perfect in following the plan set by God and because of it we are blessed.

In Genesis 6:22 we are told that Noah did all God commanded him. He chose to do the work of the Lord. He stopped all his plans and went to the mode of never-the-less not my will but thine be done. He gave up all to complete the work he was called to do. He worked on God's presentation of the ark of safety. Like Jesus he laid down his life for others.

The people did not believe. They mocked the work of the God and heeded not the warnings, and so the people perished. They did not believe the prophet and so they did not prosper.

Noah and his family was not the norm, they were considered strange and different from what had been accepted during that wicked time. Just like Jesus, he came with the plan of God. Today many do not heed the warning and reject Jesus and his work. This is why so many perish and do not prosper.

Noah believed God and so did his family. When you are chosen by God and are presenting God to others they may laugh at you and mock you. Do not allow discouragement to take a hold of you. Everyone has been given the power to choose life or death. You cannot make up someone's mind for them. It is personal decision to choose life or death.

Do what God asked you to do, and pray. You are not the one being rejected it is God and his will for their lives they are rejecting. Follow your assignment and continue to pray the will of the Father. It is his will that none be loss. Stand in the gap and intercede not for their mind to change but for their heart to change so they can receive.

You ever wonder what went through Noah's mind as he sat in the ark. Many times we fear change and yet God has us boxed in safely. This is when the spirit of worry will try to attack. All your worries is unfounded and just a mind game of the devil.

You are safe in the will of God. You may hear the horrors of others, but stay in place. Trust him as he will bring you through the floods of life. Your story does not have to end tragic or like anyone else. Noah knew that all mankind was being wiped out and he was not afraid to start over in a new world with his family. He had God on his side. What more did he need?

He was rejected by society and even called crazy but he kept working. Noah was chosen to bring change to the world. Evil was to be washed from the earth and only righteousness was to remain. He had found grace in the eyes of God. What more do you need? You will be challenged but remember you have been chosen and equipped by God.

CHOSEN TO BRING CHANGE TO THE WORLD!

CHAPTER 3

Moses

Exodus 3:9-10 reads,
"Now therefore, behold the cry of the children of Israel is come unto me: and I have also seen the oppression wherewith the Egyptians oppress them.

Come now therefore, and I will send thee unto Pharaoh, that thou mayest bring forth my people the children of Israel out of Egypt."

In Exodus 3:10 the Lord called and is sending Moses to do a particular work. In other words he is now receiving his assignment from the Lord. Moses is told to come. He needed to get closer to God. He needed to hear him clearly and he was given a time frame to do it in. It was time for him to hear Gods' plan.

In life Moses has been abandoned, rejected, and didn't fit in with the crowd (he was not an Egyptian by birth). A murderous spirit was sent to kill him at birth but God protected him. He learned to love and have compassion because of his circumstances and trials. He grew up seeing the affliction on his people and now he has killed one of the enemies by fleshy means. This murderous spirit was again sent to destroy him in another way.

You may have a passion to do what God has called you to, but be careful that you are not killing people trying to help them. You must move when God say so and in the manner he prescribes. Do not be moved by your emotions. Your emotions can get you in a mess and you will have to retreat, repent and remove your wayward walk from the presence of God and listen to what he says.

Moses had to learn how to beat that enemy by spiritual means and he needed the true and living God by his side. You cannot win a spiritual battle by fleshly means. Shake the dust off. God visited with Moses, equipped him, prepared him, and instructed him. God and his promises were with Moses. He was prepared for battle. He was guaranteed to win, and promised that he would prosper. He had to follow God's plan.

Now it was time, and he has to go back to Egypt to help his fellowmen who were still bound, rejected, in battle for their lives, and abandoned. He was sent to deliver them back to the safe keeping and care of the Lord. This is what a chosen vessel of the Lord who has been sent does. He will have a record of having defeated the enemy by supernatural means through God. They have been called and equipped to go out and war for the souls of others.

Afterwards they are to show and go with those they bring out to the safe place in God. Your life is a living testimony. How you live is very important. People will follow your example. You must be able to lead. When on your assignment it is not enough to point people to God but you go with them as well. How can you lead someone from a place of burden to a place of worship if you yourself have not been there?

Exodus 3:10
"Come now therefore, and I will send thee unto Pharaoh, that thou mayest bring forth my people the children of Israel out of Egypt."

This is the first time God had called Moses and given him a promise and an assignment. He had been chosen. We must look at Moses response because it was not as we may have expected.

Moses has been called and chosen but comes up with a few excuses of why he cannot go. All of his excuses are rooted in fear. When you hear God's plan for your life the first thing you do is fear. "What if….?" And why me?" are questions that begin to surface as fear begins to dig in.

Fear tries to control you by attacking your mind first. It will present different scenarios in your imagination. Pull those thoughts down. They do not belong in heavenly places. You must bring them subject to the word and knowledge of God. The spirit of fear will try to cause you to go AWOL from your assigned duty in order to keep the captives.

Moses was called to come and as a consequence of coming he was given a plan. God is greater and able to destroy all fear, if you let him. There is a consequence no matter which way you choose. Be wise and choose God's plan.

> Verse 11
> "And Moses said unto God, Who am I, that I should go unto Pharaoh, and that I should bring forth the children of Israel out of Egypt?"

Moses questions why God chose him. He did not want to go back to Egypt. He asked that age old question, "Why me?" Yet he was wondering what would happen If he did go back. Fear was beginning to grip him. He did not want the responsibility. He may have felt a little ashamed after watching his people toil as slaves while he enjoy the luxury of Pharaoh's house. He did not feel worthy.

He may have feared for his life, remember he did kill someone. He may have envisioned that he himself may be enslaved or killed. He began to look at the scenarios the enemy was presenting to his imagination. During that moment he forgot who God really was.

We all have at some point peeped out at situations through the eyes of fear or our own fleshy desires or emotions. Stay in the will and love of God. This is where we lay ourselves and fear down.

> *Verse 12*
> *"And he (God) said, certainly I will be with thee; and this shall be a token unto thee, that I have sent thee: when thou hast brought forth the people out of Egypt, ye shall serve God upon this mountain."*

God give assurance to Moses with a promise that he would be with him. If that was not enough he gave him notice of being with him even in the future when he completes his assignment. God let Moses know he would not fail or die but live to serve him. God promised.

> *Exodus 3:13*
> *"And Moses said unto God, Behold, when I come unto the children of Israel, and shall say unto them, The God of your*

fathers hath sent me unto you; and they shall say to me, what is his name? What shall I say unto them?"

He knew he was talking to God and so he wanted God to say his name. When God speaks to you and tells you what he is assigning you to do the first thing you do is question, is this God? Remember he was raised in Pharaoh's house and they served other gods so he still had that in his head as well. He had to try the spirit to see if it be the true God.

Make sure that you know that the true and living God is sending you and not some devilish spirit or your own human ambition. Moses question was real because the world system and teaching he was accustomed to was not the same as the Israelites. The more he talked to God the more God revealed himself to him. Prayer is necessary and a two way street. Make sure you listen and hear God too.

You must keep open communication with God before embarking on any assignment. God will reveal himself to you along with the details. He will show you the past, present and future situations if you stay before him in prayer. Hear God, listen and obey.

Do not try to figure it out. God has a plan that is infallible. Just be ready and go with what he said. Moses tried to figure out what the Israelites would question of him. He tried to imagine different scenarios again fearing failure.

God is in control not your perceptions or imagination. Let this mind be in you which was also in Christ Jesus. Jesus mind was on pleasing the Father by doing the Father's will; not on what others would say of him. In the will of God there is no failure.

> *Exodus 3:14-15*
> *"And God said unto Moses, I AM THAT I AM: and he said, thus shalt thou say unto the children of Israel, I AM hath sent me unto you.*
>
> *And God said moreover unto Moses, Thus shalt thou say to the children of Israel, the Lord God of your fathers, the God of Abraham, the God of Isaac, the God of Jacob, hath sent me unto you: this is the name forever, and this is my memorial unto all generations."*

God gives Moses a little history lesson on who he is. He tells him what to say to the children of Israel. God will give you the words to speak to whom he sends you to. He wants you to remember how he was with those who faithfully served him and that he will be with you as well. God is not a respecter of persons. If you are told to write it; then write it. If told to speak then speak it. Whatever he says, do it. Do exactly what he said and do not add to it or take away from it.

God's track record speaks for him, that he is a faithful God. The children of Israel needed to be reminded that God is faithful and had not abandoned them. Moses had to know that God did not abandon him when he was sent down the river as a baby and raised in Pharaoh's house. He had been chosen to go that path.

He had overcome and now was able to help others get delivered and set free. He was sent to help his brethren. Moses was a type of an apostle. God gave him the plan and he gave it to his team. They worked together Aaron and the Elders.

You past attacks, bondages, hurts and all the ugly things that may have happened to you has equipped you, and made you strong in the Lord and in the power of his might. You have been made ready to battle on behalf of another. You are a winner and you have been chosen. God made you just for this. In him you will not fail.

In Exodus 3:16-18 we see that Moses is told to:

1. Go (sent)
2. Gather the Elders of Israel together (unity)
3. Speak an encouraging word from the Lord to them (prophesy)
4. Let them know God has been with them and seen what they have gone through (encourage)
5. Give them God's promise to deliver them up and out of their affliction of Egypt (bring hope)
6. Bring them to a healthy and rich place (prosper)
7. God promises Moses that they will hear and obey him (submission)
8. That they shall all go both he and the elders to the king of Egypt and tell him that the God of the Hebrews has had a meeting with them. (one accord)

9. Moses is told that they shall tell the King to let them go for 3 days into the wilderness to make a sacrifice to the Lord their God. (worship)

Moses has now received his instructions of what to do, who to go to and what to say. He knows what to do with the elders and the King of Egypt. It may have seemed impossible to Moses but remember all things are possible to him that believe. Faith in what God has said for you to do is vital because there will be a trial as we find in Exodus 3:19 God says:

"And I am sure that the king of Egypt will not let you go, no, not by a mighty hand."

Just when you think it is all good, you will be tried. Hold fast to the faith and the liberty to which God has set you free. Do not turn back and do not give in. Remember God is your defense. He will make a way when there seems to be no way. Trials and tribulations will come but you are already victorious in Christ Jesus.

Exodus 3:20
"And I will stretch out my hand, and smite Egypt with all my wonders which I will do in the midst thereof: and after that he will let you go."

God will warn you of the enemy's tactics and he will then stretch forth his hand and strike for you. You will be assured of the victory and leave with the spoils. You will triumph over the enemy making a show of him openly. This battle is not yours, but it is the Lord's.

Verse 21-22
"And I will give this people favor in the sight of the Egyptians: and it shall come to pass, that, when ye go, ye shall not go empty.

But every woman shall borrow of her neighbor and of her that sojourneth in her house, jewels of silver, and jewels of gold, and raiment: and ye shall put them upon your sons, and upon your daughters; and ye shall spoil the Egyptians."

You will not leave those places of bondage, hurt, rejection, and pain just okay. You will leave with jewels of wisdom, peace, and understanding. You will come out with gold and silver, covered in the glory of God's redemption and rewards. God promise that you will come out and be a living testimony of his favor and power. He is the same God yesterday, today and forever more.

Moses realized he already had the victory and because of his obedience others would be blessed beyond measure. Your suffering is not in vain. It will help groom you. Others will get to know of your God and his ability to deliver them. They will follow you as you follow God. This is the laying down of your life to help another. You lead by example.

Jesus did this for you and me. He was sent to go into a place where he was scorned. When he came on a personal level with mankind, he was rejected. He told the world that the Great I AM sent him to deliver man from all evil.

He came unto his own and they received him not. He continued to do the works of the Father. The Father displayed his wondrous miracles to the world yet they still crucified him. Even as he was dying he stood in the breach asking the Father to forgive them for they knew not what they were doing.

Jesus died to his flesh but rose up in heavenly places having defeated death, the horrors of the grave and all manner of evil. He defeated that murderous spirit that had been after what God loved so much, man. He made a way for mankind who was bound and enslaved to come out from the wicked desires of the enemy. Jesus bought mankind through salvation to a place of prosperity and love. He reconnected mankind back to God, and because he lives we can live again.

Moses had to die out to his fleshy desires and rise up in the power of God to save his people. Moses was sent down the river into Pharaoh's house as a babe. He was carried on the water of the spirit to his destiny. There his people was enslaved and in bondage. He grew and excelled in a place of pain and sorrows. He loved his people yet they did not receive him because he did look like them.

Moses had to go up to a meeting with God and then go back to the place of pain and sorrow to deliver what God loves, his people. Moses came back not in his regalia but lowly looking just like the children of Israel. Your sorrow and pain (testimony) has a purpose to bring deliverance, healing and salvation to others.

Moses foreshadows Jesus. Like Jesus he:

1. had a place of prominence
2. he has a meeting with the Father
3. he was sent out
4. he was sought after to be killed at birth
5. he saw the atrocities that the enemy afflicted on his people
6. he came having shed his divinity (regalia)
7. he takes on the look of the people he is sent to
8. he is tempted but gets to the nevertheless place
9. he puts the will of the Father over his own will
10. he has a meeting with the enemy
11. he takes the authority over the enemy
12. he will destroy the very last enemy
13. he does miraculous works
14. he heals and saves the people restoring wholeness to them
15. he made a way out of no way
16. he brings them to a land flowing with milk and honey.
17. God receives him when his assignment is over

You also have been chosen to lay down your life for another so that God would be glorified and your brethren delivered from the ravages of sin, sickness and death. You can do all things through Christ that sent and strengthens you.

Stop looking for excuses. Do what God said, and do what God has assigned to you. Don't you want to hear "welcome home thy good and faithful servant"?

Follow the pattern.

- Pray

- Listen to God's direction
- Go forth
- Fear not
- Know your faith will be tested
- Reside at Never-the-less not your will
- Expect God to intervene (Miracles)
- Be a living example
- Bring others out
- Complete your assignment

Stop making excuses when God is sending you out. He is almighty and able to complete what he has started in you. Do not allow your own thinking to get in the way of God. In Exodus 4:1, Moses says to God that they will not believe him or listen to him and will say that God has not sent him. Then in verse 10 he starts comparing himself to others saying he cannot speak eloquent but is of a slow speech and not able to speak well.

Do not worry how you will say and what you will say. God just want you to open your mouth and he will speak for you. Aaron was another man's voice. When you begin to speak what God told you they will not hear you but will hear God speaking through you.

> *Exodus 4:11-12*
> *"And the Lord said unto him, who hath made man's mouth? Or who maketh the dumb, or deaf, or the seeing, or the blind? Have not I the Lord?*

Now therefore go, and I will be with thy mouth, and teach thee what thou shalt say."

God again tells Moses to go a second time, after basically telling him to cut out the excuses I am with you. Moses not wanting to go tries to bring another excuse. Now the Lord gets angry and sends Aaron with Moses to speak for him. Once more Moses try to get excused by asking his father in law if he could leave to see if his brethren was still alive knowing that is not why he was going. His father in law tells him to go in peace. No hindrance from him.

Don't try to get excused from your assignment. If God called and chose you then he knows exactly what you can and cannot do. This is a form of rebellion and fear is the root of it. Where is your faith now? Did you not tell God to use you?

In Exodus 4:19, God tells Moses again to go for the third time, knowing he was afraid for his life. In his patience God assures him that those who sort after his life are dead, Past tense. It had already been taken care of. You do not want to bring trouble to yourself.

Be obedient. You may have to go through a situation as a test of your faith. You will learn from it and remember to go when you are told. Some troubles we bring on ourselves not heeding the first warning or calling of the Lord.

Moses questioned God's ability because of his own inability. Moses sorts first the approval of man to go and do what God had told him to. If God say Go, Go! You do not want to anger God or test his patience.

As stated earlier when the Lord has called and chosen you fear will attack. Moses did not want to go because he was afraid he would be killed. He was afraid that no one would believe or accept him coming to them in the name of the God of Israel.

Moses was raised and schooled, dressed like and looked like the Egyptians. They would remember him as Pharaoh's adopted brother. Moses feared that Pharaoh would mock him and possibly order his death. He was afraid of man, when he should have feared I AM that I AM—God.

Most often people will reject you because they will be judging the book by its cover. They will see all the mess you been through and not see the God who delivered you.

You are sent with the sign of the chosen one wearing the rejection and troubles of the past. Your tragedies, trials, and troubles signify that you have been chosen for the job. It is this foolish thing that will confound those with earthly wisdom.

Moses and Aaron just two men against the armies of pharaoh probably looked pretty weak but with God all things are possible. Together with the Lord they would confound those who thought themselves mighty.

One more thing in Ex. 4:12 the Lord tells Moses he will teach him what he shall say. That means he had to learn something.

He had to be tested on it and pass the test so as to remember the knowledge gained from it. I don't care how horrible the situation or how tough the test, look for the good in it. God allowed you to go through it and therefore God being good, (being=continuing to be forever good) has put some good to it.

How horrible it must have been for Moses to learn that he was sent down the river by his mother to save his life and he wound up separated from his family. He then was adopted by the ones who were abusing his family and kindred. Now see the good! Look for it. Learn! That horrible situation worked out for the good of so many others.

> *In Psalms 106:23:*
> *"Therefore he said that he would destroy them, had not Moses his chosen stood before him in the breach, to turn away the wrath, lest he should destroy them."*

When you have been chosen you have a grace that can change the mind of God. God was about to destroy the very ones he sent Moses to deliver from bondage. They had forgotten what God had done for them. How he saved them from those that hated them but he did not destroy them.

Moses was a chosen prepared vessel sent to bring deliverance to the people and God remembered the covenant that was made. Like Moses you have been chosen to stand in the gap for others who may have fallen prey to the enemy's devices. God will hear the intercessory prayer and have mercy.

It is not just enough to go and do what God has told you to do but to also keep a watch in prayer knowing that the enemy will try again to bring them into bondage. They may forget what God has done and or brought them from and backslide.

Have you ever wondered how someone whom God has delivered from a horrible situation through his miraculous work turn back to the same sinful ways? They do so because they forgot God and what he has done. They get comfortable in where they are at. They forget what it took to get them there.

Lessons to remember; do not forget the one God used to get you out. Do not forget where you came from. Do not forget the Word of God. Do not forget your saviour who was sent to deliver you. Do not forget the council of the Lord.

Being chosen and sent you can change the atmosphere of death and destruction to one of mercy, deliverance and salvation. Moses not only physically did the work of the Lord but even in his prayers he continued to keep a watch over God's people and bring deliverance miraculously by the Lord. He prayed and God said he would not destroy them. Moses stood in the breach and God turned away his wrath. Your standing in the breach may be the difference between life and death.

God made good on all his promises to Moses. Moses was able to successfully execute his assignment and get the children of Israel out of the hand of bondage. Moses was chosen to change the whole atmosphere of Egypt. Poverty, slavery, hopelessness, murder, bondage, hatred, abandonment, rejection, pain, hurt, idolatry, and fear all had to bow to the Lord. Moses had been delivered first and then went back to help others. Your suffering is not in vain, it is a tool of strength in the hands of God. You have been chosen!

CHOSEN TO BRING DELIVERANCE!

CHAPTER 4

Aaron

In Exodus 4:14-17 it states:
"And the anger of the Lord was kindled against Moses, and he said, is not Aaron the Levite thy brother? I know that he can speak well. And also, behold he cometh forth to meet thee: and when he seeth thee, he will be glad in his heart.

And thou shalt speak unto him, and put words in his mouth: and I will be with thy mouth, and with his mouth, and will teach you what ye shall do.

And he shall be thy spokesman unto the people: and he shall be, even he shall be to thee instead of a mouth, and thou shalt be to him instead of God.

And thou shalt take this rod in thine hand, wherewith thou shalt do signs."

Aaron was chosen by God to be a spokesman for Moses. He would be a mouthpiece to speak forth God's words. The first thing God told Aaron to do was to go into the wilderness to meet Moses. He met Moses in the wilderness, on the mount of God and there he greeted him. Moses told Aaron all the words of the Lord who had sent him and all the signs which he had commanded him.

Aaron spoke all the words that the Lord had spoken to Moses and did the signs in the sight of the people. The people believed and they bowed their heads in worship. The signs followed the word of the Lord. Further in chapter 5 of Exodus you will see that both Aaron and Moses spoke to Pharaoh. Signs are for the unbeliever.

Both Aaron and Moses operated as one. They were in agreement and on one accord. Moses was made a god to pharaoh and Aaron was as Moses his prophet. They worked together as a team.

> Exodus 7:1,
> "And the Lord said unto Moses, See, I have made thee a god
> to pharaoh: and Aaron thy brother shall be thy prophet."

The prophet is sent by God and should work in conjunction with the apostle. Both are called and sent to work together. We will see in the following chapters that Aaron spoke and then he would stretch forth his rod. Signs would be wrought following the word of God. This prophet was chosen by God, called and sent.

Pharaoh asked Moses to pray and ask God to remove the plagues. He agreed to comply with what Moses had asked of him. Pharaoh's heart hardened and he then refused to comply. This happened over and over again. Moses prayed for the Egyptians when pharaoh asked and also for the Israelites who were enslaved.

God instructs Moses what to say and Moses would tell Aaron and they would then speak to Pharaoh. A sign from God would always follow. There must be unity in the spirit in leadership.

Remember that Moses is a type of an apostle. Apostles are able to move the hand of God through prayer. They are able to stand in the gap for the sinner and the saint. They cannot have respect of persons and must intercede for all. Apostles will go the distance in intercession that God will turn away his wrath.

Jesus came to save all who were in need and lost. He died for all people everywhere. He prays to the Father in intercession on our behalf standing in the gap. Moses was a shadow of Christ in that instance.

Although Moses may have been hurt to see the suffering of his fellowman, he yet prayed for mercy for the just and the unjust. He would go to the Father on behalf of pharaoh and the Egyptians for mercy for them both.

With Jesus there is no respect of person and God's mercy is available for the just and the unjust. It is not the will of the Father that any be lost. Jesus went the distance even to the point of death to his desires and his will lined up with the will of the Father. Are you willing to lay down your life and die out to your desires for another?

God gave ample space for pharaoh to surrender to him. Eventually the bondage is broken off the Israelites, and their enemy must free them. They cross the Red Sea and all seems to be going well. You know how the story goes.

Time go on and Moses has gone up the mount again but this time he stays a bit longer and the people begin to entice the prophet Aaron to make them gods. So let us get back to Aaron a type of prophet who is called and chosen who is accepted as long as he can please the people and give them what they want when they want it.

> Exodus 32:1-5,
> "And when the people saw that Moses delayed to come down out of the mount, the people gathered themselves together unto Aaron, and said unto him, up, make us gods, which shall go before us; for as for this Moses, the man that brought us up out of the land of Egypt, we wot not what is become of him.
>
> And Aaron said unto them, break off the golden earrings, which are in the ears of your wives, of your sons, and of your daughters, and bring them unto me.
>
> And all the people brake off the golden earrings which were in the ears, and brought them unto Aaron.
>
> And he received them at their hand, and fashioned it with a graving tool, after he had made it a molten calf: and they said, these be thy gods, O Israel, which brought thee up out of the land of Egypt.
>
> And Aaron saw it and built an altar before it: and Aaron made proclamation and said, tomorrow is a feast to the Lord."

Prophets beware of the people who pull at you for a "word from the Lord" and God has not spoken. Do not proclaim something God has not said, just to be accepted. You were not chosen for that.

Aaron received the people's gold and he made unto them a false god. He shaped it and built an altar so they could worship before it. He wanted the approval of the people so bad that he was willing to sin and make a proclamation that God did not authorize.

He felt the rejection as the people began to wonder where Moses was. Aaron did not have a word from the Lord because he was the mouthpiece for Moses and Moses was still up on the mountain. Aaron was in a dry season feeling rejected so he decided to give the people what they wanted but to do that he had to turn himself over to a false god. In doing this he led the people astray with a false word and false worship.

If you speak a word to the people and it is not from God and the people receive it and rejoice over it, you have led them astray. They have received a false word from another which is idolatry. As they worship a false god for a false word; they are now worshipping not in the right spirit and not in truth.

Aaron took what was valuable; what the Lord had blessed the people to come out of Egypt with. He took their worship of God, their gold and used it to turn them away from God and to steal some glory. He took it to get some recognition. He was out of order and had led God's people astray. He did not warn them that they should wait on the Lord. Out of fear of rejection he himself did not wait to hear from God.

Prophets be careful that when there is no word from the Lord, and you are in what seems to be a dry season, that you do not try to please the crowd with your own proclamations. It brings the people into a false worship unto a man-made god. This put the people in danger of death and destruction.

You bring them to sin and shame and uncover them. Their blood will be required at your hands. Prophet you have been chosen to bring change but make sure you are bringing life and not death. Wait for God's instruction.

This is a warning remember you have been chosen.

CHOSEN TO SPEAK LIFE!

CHAPTER 5

Leah

Often women are overlooked to stand in significant places in society. I feel that it is not that women are overlooked but that they have been left out of many equations that had powerful outcomes. I believe that we have focused on what the men have done more than women.

Today we are going to look at Leah. We all may know the story of being the one that was not so beautiful and helped trick a man into marrying her. I want to look a little deeper at this woman who was so rejected that even her father used her as a pawn for his own selfish gain.

This woman suffered much rejection from her Father, her husband, and her sister. The bible tells us she was not loved, she was not good to look upon, and that she even was hated. She was given to be sexually exploited and made to be a lie. She was attacked by a competitive and jealous spirit. Yet, God saw her and loved her, and blessed her so that Jesus Christ would come through her bloodline.

I want to carefully examine the words in the scripture and see what is happening. Get a picture of the scene as it unfolds and look deeper than the surface and go into the emotions of the individuals. See the toll it must have taken on her children as they grew up knowing their father did not love their mother. See the competition and the hatred spilling out between the sisters. Look and look again, Behold!

Genesis 29:15-31:
"And Laban said unto Jacob, because thou art my brother, shouldest thou therefore serve me for naught? Tell me, what shall thou wages be?

And Laban had two daughters: the name of the elder was Leah, and the name of the younger was Rachel.

Leah was tender eyed; but Rachel was beautiful and well-favored.

And Jacob loved Rachel; and said, I will serve thee seven years for Rachel thy younger daughter.

And Laban said it is better that I give her to thee, than that I should give her to another man: abide with me.

And Jacob severed seven years for Rachel; and they seemed unto him but a few days, for the love he had to her.

And Jacob said unto Laban; give me my wife, for my days are fulfilled, that I may go in unto her.

And Laban gathered together all the men of the place, and made a feast.

And it came to pass in the evening that he took Leah his daughter, and brought her to him; and he went in unto her.

And Laban gave unto his daughter Leah Zilpah his maid for an handmaid.

And it came to pass that in the morning, behold it was Leah: and he said unto Laban, What is this thou has done unto me? Did not I serve with thee for Rachel? Wherefore then hast thou beguiled me?

And Laban said it must not be so done in our country, to give the younger before the firstborn.

Fulfill her week, and we will give thee this also for the service which thou shalt serve with me yet seven other years,

And Jacob did so, and fulfilled her week: and he gave him Rachel his daughter to wife also.

And Laban gave to Rachel his daughter Bilhah his handmaid to be her maid.

And he went in also unto Rachel, and he loved also Rachel more than Leah, and served with him yet seven other years.

And when the Lord saw that Leah was hated, he opened her womb; but Rachel was barren."

Leah's name meant weary or causing dissatisfaction according to Webster. I just want to point out also Laban gave his maid which was usually a young unmarried servant that often was a virgin, really like a child to be a handmaid for Leah. He gave her an inexperienced child to serve her and to help her deliver children and give her advice. Rachel got the opposite. She got an experienced handmaid to help and advise her and do chores as needed.

Leah was rejected, unwanted, and unloved by her own husband, father and sister. She did not know what it was to be loved truly by a man. She had to feel a sense of longing and loneliness. All she had was her children to keep her smiling. Can you see her face knowing she was used as a pawn to deceive and hating on herself because she was not as pretty and wanted as her sister? This was now her life, so she thought for the rest of her days.

Can you see the spirit of division pulling this family apart and that even the children are affected to some degree. Sibling rivalry, wounded spirits, grief and depression were a constant daily deal. All this hurt Leah had. I can also see Rachel with her own set of pain having to share the man she loved and knowing her sister loved him too and yet barren for a while.

The first seven years Leah had an edge over her sister yet she knew that it was going to go from bad to worse soon. For the rest of her life as the seven years would come to an end she knew Jacob would be happily in love but not with her. The thought of what was to come had to haunt her daily as she looked at her sister.

Further in the scripture, Leah was put out on the front line by Jacob as he feared his brother Esau's retaliation. She and her children with the servants and their children were out on the frontline while Rachel and her child was kept back and covered for safekeeping.

Jacob felt Leah and her children were just as expendable as the servants but not his beloved Rachel and Joseph. I imagine the hurt of being uncovered and unprotected by the man she loved who never loved her back; another dagger to the heart.

Leah was fertile and bore five sons and one daughter for Jacob. She gave her handmaid to him as a wife who bore him two sons. Rachel gives her maid as well who bore sons. Eventually

Rachel's womb is opened and she bears two sons dying after childbirth with the second child. Jacob now has four wives and a troop of children. Rachel and Leah are having their battles and striving with one another for his affection.

Finally Leah gives up after giving birth to Judah from the works of the flesh and symbolically turns her affection to the praise and honor of God. She remained faithful and devoted to her husband.

Being fertile meant she had favor with God and she knew it, and named her son Judah. Now she will praise the Lord and leave childbearing; a work of the flesh. It was time to move from fleshy works and seeking the praise of man to allowing the will of God to be manifested in her life.

Leah was rejected by men but chosen by God. She suffered much rejection and so did Christ Jesus. We are told that if we suffer with him we shall reign with him. Like Leah we have to come to a place where although we are persecuted and have to go through many trials, to birth the promises of God. If you need help, do not give up use what you got to produce. Leah used Zilpah to give birth to Gad and Asher.

I do not want to leave Rachel seemingly like the villain in this story but I wanted to look at Leah more specifically. Rachel also birthed great men for the tribe of Israel but I do want to note that she had hidden old pagan gods under her and bought a generational curse on herself.

She was in a polygamous marriage but she also served more than one god as well. She held on to superstition and paganist ideas in her heart. Jacob did not know until he found the hidden idols and removed and buried them. Rachel is another story to tell.

Leah a major founder of the tribes of Israel was favored by the Lord. He saw her hurt, he saw the hatred towards her and he blessed her. She may have been marred by manipulation and deception but she was fulfilled by being a mother. She birthed a nation and through the lineage of Judah Jesus Christ himself came. From so much rejection comes the love of God to bring healing to all. Your suffering is not in vain.

Like Leah we as the people of God need to get to the place where our focused is not so much on what we can do in ourselves. It is not by works but by faith. We need to get our eyes off man and look to God and praise him for his goodness, knowing that all things will work together for the good. When Leah shifted her focus to God there was no more competition or strife. Life got easier as she now could rest in the love of God. Rejected by men but chosen by God!

Isaiah 54:5-6:

"For thy Maker is thine husband; the Lord of hosts is his name; and thy redeemer the Holy One of Israel; The God of the whole earth shall he be called.

For the Lord hath called thee as a woman forsaken and grieved in the spirit, and a wife of youth, when thou wast refused, saith thy God."

CHOSEN TO BE LOVED!

CHAPTER 6
Abimelech

Genesis 20:1-7
"And Abraham journeyed from thence toward the south country, and dwelled between Kadesh and Shur, and sojourned in Gerar.

And Abraham said of Sarah his wife, she is my sister: and Abimelech king of Gerar sent, and took Sarah.

But God came to Abimelech in a dream by night, and said unto him, Behold; thou art but a dead man, for the woman which thou hast taken; for she is a man's wife.

But Abimelech had not come near her: and he said Lord, wilt thou slay also a righteous nation?

Said he not unto me, She is my sister? And she, even she herself said, He is my brother: in the integrity of my heart and the innocency of my hands have I done this.

And God said unto him in a dream, Yea, I know that thou didst this in the integrity of thy heart; for I also withheld thee from sinning against me: therefore suffered I thee not to touch her.

Now therefore restore the man his wife; for he is a prophet, and he shall pray for thee, and thou shalt live: and if thou restore her not, know that thou shalt surely die, thou, and all that are thine.

Abimelech name meant father of the king but most think that this name was a title for the king of Gerar a town of Philistia. Abraham not telling the whole truth told a half truth about his half-sister failing to mention that she was also his wife. He informed the King Abimelech that Sarah was his sister and uncovered his wife.

Both husband and wife need to be on one accord in truth to keep the enemy out. Sarah also told a half truth in agreement with her husband. Abraham loved his wife but not as much as he loved his own life. Until a man is willing to give up his own life for his wife and her honor, the door is open wide for deception and enemy intrusion. This is another subject to think about.

Abraham uncovers Sarah and leaves her exposed to the wickedness of a pagan king. Abraham chose not to lay down his life for her. He thought he would not live if the king knew that she was his wife. He thought he would kill him if the king knew the full truth.

By justifying through his own reasoning he also proves he is not trusting God to protect them both. Abraham was guided by his own selfish fear of losing his life that he chose to lose Sarah instead, but God had a greater plan.

Abimelech was a pagan king with integrity and took Sarah into his harem. God restrains the king from defiling her by covering her himself through a dream. In doing so he poured out his mercy and kept the King from sinning against Him. In the dream God warns Abimelech that he has made a deadly mistake in taking another man's wife and to restore the prophet his wife.

Abimelech heeded the warning of the Lord, and the prophet Abraham had to pray for the king's life and his household. All the women had been stricken with barrenness because of this sin caused by Abrahams misleading.

He now had to cover his wife and cover the king and his kingdom with prayer. If he had prayed and trusted God in the first place all this drama could have been avoided. Needless to say the king and his house were restored.

Prophets cannot withhold truth. It is dangerous and could cause death to a generation unknowingly. Please tell the truth, the whole truth and nothing but the truth so help you God.

After learning that she indeed was Abraham's wife the king now rebukes Abraham and restores honor to Sarah. He reproves her also. Abraham the prophet is rebuked by a pagan king.

God chose this pagan king whom Abraham had rejected to now correct the prophet who crossed the line. By the king returning Sarah unharmed it caused his household to be healed and preserved his generations. This also allowed his generations to have a choice to serve the true and living God. Abimelech not only returns her whole he also blesses them with gifts and care while in the land.

We have to be mindful not to throw people away because we think they are not God fearing people. We are to love thy neighbor as thyself. From this chapter we learn that as Christians we cannot look down on non-Christians.

We are to care for all people Christian or not. We are to raise their sight to see God in how we live and how we represent Him. Speak truth and live truth. Being chosen means you will set an example for others to follow.

Allow God to convict them. It is not for you to pass judgment. There are many non-Christians that do have integrity as this chapter shows. God will have mercy on whom he will have mercy.

> *Matthew 5:43-48:*
> *"Ye have heard that it hath been said, thou shalt love thy neighbor, and hate thine enemy,*
>
> *But I say unto you, Love your enemies, bless them that curse you, do good to them that hate you, and pray for them which despitefully use you, and persecute you.*
>
> *That ye may be the children of your Father which is in heaven: for he maketh his sun to rise on the evil and on the good, and sendeth rain on the just and on the unjust.*
>
> *For if ye love them which love you, what reward have ye? Do not even the publicans the same?*
>
> *And if ye salute your brethren only, what do ye more than others? Do not even the publicans so?*
>
> *Be ye therefore perfect, even as your Father which is in heaven is perfect."*

God chose a reject to bring integrity to the prophet. Be careful of who you say is or isn't godly and by all means practice what you preach. We are to walk by faith which means to trust and believe that God will take care of our every situation. Turn it over to him. Sometimes you think long and your thinking is wrong. God can handle your most feared situation, but you must be willing to let go and let God have it. Abimelech was a chosen reject.

CHOSEN TO KNOW THE TRUTH!

CHAPTER 7
Joseph

Joseph was the son of Jacob and Rachel and his name meant, "May God add or increase". He was sold into slavery by his own brothers. He had it hard but God was with him all the way for he had been chosen.

> Genesis 37:3-4
> "Now Israel loved Joseph more than all his children, because he was the son of his old age: and he made him a coat of many colors.
>
> And when his brethren saw that their father loved him more than all his brethren, they hated him, and could not speak peaceably unto him."

Jacob is also called Israel. Joseph's mother Rachel was Jacobs's love of his life. He had been tricked into marrying her sister Leah who bore him numerous sons. Can you see how Leah's children watched how their dad favored Rachel and Joseph over them and their mother? Can you see them growing up with anger which came from competition, sibling rivalry and favoritism? They hated their own brother.

> Genesis 37:18
> "And when they saw him afar off, even before he came near unto them, they conspired against him to slay him."

Joseph the dreamer who appears to have a dream of grandeur but yet it was a very prophetic dream of what was to come. Jacob rebukes him yet observes the saying, but His brothers are full of envy toward him. Joseph is sent out to check on his brother's welfare while they were out feeding the flock by his father. His brothers first conspire together to kill him when they see him in the field approaching them. Reuben tells them not to kill him but put him in a pit hoping to save him later and bring him back to their father.

Hurt people hurt people. They were hurt because of their father's favoritism towards Joseph and so they lashed out against what he loved more.

The brothers stripped Joseph of the coat of many colors his father had covered him with. When I see this, I see the coat of pride that Jacobs laid on him. A peacock has many beautiful colors and this coat was made by his father. Pride was laid and shaped just for him. He was covered in pride and pride thinks all is well and cannot see itself. Poor Joseph had no idea of how he looked to his other siblings and if he did, he did not care because he had his father's favor.

Reuben goes to get him out of the pit and find that the other brothers had already sold him off. They chose to sell him into slavery to Egypt receiving 20 pieces of silver from a band of Ishmaelite's. They faked Joseph's death and presented that to their father causing him hurt, pain, and sorrow. Now imagine what could have been going through the heart and mind of Joseph.

Most times when we hear of rejection happening among family members someone is calling someone else the "black sheep of the family." Being called this could mean for Joseph that he:

- was odd and saw things differently than the others

- stood out as dramatic
- looked on as less than by his brothers
- his brothers were not pleased with his existence
- he had a different lifestyle, a dreamer, independent
- he has a bad reputation for being dads favorite
- he was the center of arguments amongst them
- didn't fit in with the others
- he tend to trigger the brothers wrath.

To Jacob, Joseph was the golden child. His champion and nothing he could do was ever wrong. He got the most attention from Jacob and Rachel. They helped boost his ego and made him an idol. God said you will have no other god before me and he will bring down pride. Needless to say the golden child was sold by his brothers into slavery.

Before God can use you as his chosen one you will suffer many things. Pride will be broken off and you will never desire to touch God's glory.
God allows situations to birth humility and obedience in you. You will learn to continue to serve him standing against the wiles of the devil. God will give you favor and grace to go through it all.

After you pass your training then you will be bought forth to reign. You will no longer look at those harsh situations with vengeful eyes but you will see the good. You will be able to say," it was good for me." You will be changed, and able to show others the love of God.

God will prepare a table before you in the presence of your enemies. You will sit down and break bread together, laying down your life; rewarding them good for the evil they commit against you. That is what Jesus would do.

Joseph was chosen for a particular time to come. He would be the one who would stand in the gap for his family and bring deliverance. He was the one who his parents sheltered trying to keep him from adversity. He would suffer so much. There was a purpose to all this and he had been warned in the dream. Pride blinded him to the fact it would not be so simple or easy. Pride had to be broken for humility to rise.

Humility starts by being obedient to others. Joseph as a slave had to do what he was told. He did that and more. He began to offer his assistance to help his slave master. He lays down his life, talents, and gifts to help better others.

His service was no longer a burden but he was now willing. When you have been chosen you go from just obedience to total sell out. You stop fighting against your maker and begin to seek to please him.

Joseph was ambushed first by his own father and mother by them idolizing him and showing favoritism to him. They grew him up in pride causing the other sibling to hate him enough to get rid of him. Poor Joseph was just a pawn of love and then of hate. He was enslaved by parents to be the golden child and then by his brothers as the black sheep of the family, and finally by an evil world system. Thank God for purpose even when you cannot see or understand it.

Joseph was used by God to save his family and others with the wisdom given to him by God. He acquires Egypt's wealth through obedience and promotion. What his brothers saw as a curse now they see as the blessing. He was the one they rejected and threw in the ground but God raised him up. He was chosen.

God chose him before his flesh was put under subjection to raise him up with power. He would be a blessing to his brethren supplying their need. Joseph like Jesus although he was rejected fulfills his purpose, being chosen by God. Joseph not only helped save the Egyptians but also his generations. God has no respect of person and has mercy for the just as well as the unjust according to his will.

I pray you are able to see the good in all that you have been allowed to experience. You are still here and God has not made a mistake. You may be looked upon as the "black sheep" but God's light will reveal the truth of who you are in him. You have purpose to fulfill and there are others who need you. You have been chosen!

CHOSEN TO STAND IN THE GAP!

CHAPTER 8
David

I Samuel 13:13-14

"And Samuel said to Saul, Thou hast done foolishly: thou hast not kept the commandment of the Lord thy God, which he commanded thee: for now would the Lord have established thy kingdom upon Israel forever.

But now thy kingdom shall not continue: the Lord hath sought him a man after his own heart, and the Lord hath commanded him to be captain over his people, because thou hast not kept that which the Lord commanded thee."

As Saul was tumbling from grace; God was searching for a man after his own heart. Remember that the people had rejected the leadership of God for that of a king. They chose to set a man to lead them. God being rejected again by his created man allows them to have a king and tell them where to find him. Saul had hid among stuff. The people saw him as a great, tall leader and warrior and said, God save the king.

Samuel then told them the manner of the kingdom, wrote it in a book, placed it before the Lord, and sent all the people home. Saul left as well, he had been chosen and the spirit of the Lord would come upon him anointing him for service as king. Soon he began to break away from the ordinances of God. God then begins searching for someone who has a heart like his. God is looking for a good shepherd.

In Ezekiel 34:11 he states

> *"For thus saith the Lord God; Behold, I, even I, will both search my sheep, and seek them out."*

Ezekiel is speaking a word of woe from God to the shepherds who did not feed, care for, or offer healing to God's sheep. As the good shepherd he promises restoration to the sheep and full accountability of their welfare from the shepherds. God is searching for one with a heart like his.

In Ezekiel 34:21-22 God says:

"Because ye have thrust with side and with shoulder, and pushed all the diseased with your horns, till ye have scattered them abroad;

Therefore I will save my flock, and they shall no more be a prey; and I will judge between cattle and cattle.

I decided to search what a shepherd does. Look at what I found naturally and spiritually:

- The shepherd loves his sheep so that he will sacrifice himself for them.
- The shepherd will have an intimate relationship with his sheep.
- They will get special attention care and love, and he will know their cry of pain, fear, and joy.
- The shepherd understands the needs of his sheep both individually and corporately.
- The shepherd knows what makes the sheep sick and what a threat to them is, keeping them from unclean and profane things.
- The shepherd protects and secures the sheep from outside predators, and is willing to war on behalf of the sheep.

- The shepherd will lead the sheep into fresh pasture and fresh water.
- The shepherd must study and receive fresh manna to feed the flock.
- The shepherd goes before the sheep leading them, you cannot tell them to go where you have not gone before them.

- The sheep know their shepherds voice and will not follow another.
- The sheep cannot live without their shepherd; they will become lost or prey without them.
- The sheep trust their shepherd and that is why they follow them.
- There are boundaries set to keep the sheep safe and together.

- They are in a pen on one accord with the shepherd keeping watch.
- The shepherd does not give up on his investment, he has plans for them.
- The shepherd will make personal sacrifices for his sheep.
- David did not run or hide but fought off the bear and the lion.
- Because sheep do not naturally shed they need to be sheared every now and then to keep them clean and healthy.

- The shepherd and his sheep will have the same smell.

- Shepherds will use their staff to pull to safety or nudge a sheep towards the path it should go with a gentle push.
- The Holy Spirit nudges us in our spirit in the way that God would have us to go and pull us out of a mess with the word.

- If a sheep constantly wanders the shepherd will break the leg of the sheep and carry them while they heal taking care of them and providing for them and when they are well again they will have learned to trust and depend on the shepherd and follow his voice.
- Sometimes God will allow adversity to come to chastise a wayward sheep and that sheep will learn to trust God and hear him. As God brings healing to the outward man, he also is comforting the inner man and carrying him through the tough times of learning.
- The shepherd has a future vision for his sheep.

God was looking for a man after his own heart that would care, heal, feed, and protect his sheep. He seeks one who would sacrifice their life for them. He found David who is a type of Jesus. David was chosen by God.

Remember in I Samuel chapter 16, Samuel went to find the one God had chosen. He was sent by God to the house of Jesse to anoint the one who would be king. Jesse called his sons forward and the prophet began to look naturally and God tells him not to do that.

I Samuel 16:7
"But the Lord said unto Samuel, Look not on his countenance, or on the height of his stature; because I have

refused him: for the Lord seeth not as man seeth; for man
looketh on the outward appearance, but the Lord looketh
on the heart."

Jesse presents seven sons and God did not choose any of them.
He presented them twice and Samuel asks him is this it?

I Samuel 16:11-13
"And Samuel said unto Jesse, Are here all thy children? And
he said, there remaineth yet the youngest, and, behold, he
keepeth the sheep. And Samuel said unto Jesse, send and
fetch him: for we will not sit down till he come hither.

And he sent, and brought him in. Now he was ruddy, and
withal of a beautiful countenance, and goodly to look to.
And the Lord said, arise, anoint him: for this is he.

Then Samuel took the horn of oil, and anointed him in
the midst of his brethren: and the Spirit of the Lord came
upon David from that day forward. So Samuel rose up,
and went to Ramah."

David was to his father and brethren just a small runt. How
could this weak child be called as king? He stank like sheep,
his skin was sunburnt but beside that, he was handsome.
His brothers were tall warriors, but David was just a faithful
shepherd. He was anointed and the Spirit of God came on
him too.

You can imagine how his brothers and father must have felt.
Yes, they had to be confounded. God had chosen David the
weakest to confound the mighty.

During his time of training his inner man was being built. His trust in God was being established and he knew he was able to slay the bear and lion only by the power of God. He did not run, he stood and fought. He protected his sheep with his life trusting God to help him. David could carry a sheep but besides that he was not a physically trained warrior. He could not even wear the armor of a man.

The devil tried to kill David through King Saul when the spirit of jealousy rose up in him. David never retaliated although opportunity was there. He refused to step out of the will of God. God was his defense. David even confronted a giant with just a sling and stones and defeated him in the name of the Lord. You know the story of David and Goliath.

> *Ezekiel 34:23-24*
> *"And I will set up one shepherd over them, and he shall feed them, even my servant David; he shall feed them, and he shall be their shepherd.*
>
> *And I the Lord will be their God, and my servant David a prince among them; I the Lord have spoken it."*

David was rejected because he did not look the part. He was small and not trained in warfare. He could not even wear armor. His family never, ever considered him to be nothing more than a shepherd. They never thought that God could use him in such a mighty way.

Others may not understand how God can choose you and use you for his glory. You are the one that everyone has given up on. You are the one, who is simple yet faithful in that dirty low paying job; always looked over for a better position. You are the one that your family said would never amount to anything. You who look good but they say is only good for making music. Yes you! God has chosen you.

Like David God has chosen you to a place of greater authority and rule. God chose you to slay giants that are in the lives of his people. Man has judged you by your outward appearance. God saw your heart and it looked like his and said, "That is the one." David had been chosen and so have you.

CHOSEN TO LEAD!

CHAPTER 9

Widow Of Zarephath

In I Kings chapter 17 we see the story of the prophet Elijah being sent to Zarephath by the Lord. The Lord had already prepared the heart of a widow to sustain him. Previously the Lord sustained him by a brook of Cherith with ravens who brought him food. There came a drought and now God was sending him to another place.

In Zarephath there was a gentile widow who had lost her husband and was in a famine. She had a young son as well. She was down to her last bit of oil and meal and went out to gather sticks. She had already given up and accepted the fact this would be their last meal and then they would die.

The prophet Elijah arrives sees the widow and asks for water. As the widow is going to get the water he asks her for a piece of bread too. At this point she describes to him what she truthfully has. She only has enough meal for herself and her son's last meal before they die.

She had no idea that she and her son had been chosen to live. Now the prophet gives her a prophetic word that she would not run out of oil or meal if she made a cake also for him. She would have divine supply until the rain came. She followed the word of the prophet and ate many days and lived.

When you feel helpless and alone and abandoned by all who cared, do not give up on the word of God. God promises to sustain you and keep you when man is gone. This widow's son may have been too young to work to help bring in what they needed after her husband had died. She had no man to help her and she was prepared to die.

You may be feeling rejected and helpless and ready to just give up. Don't let your dreams die, the Lord has a plan for you. It is not over. God has chosen you to live and give life. This woman gave all as a sacrifice to the prophet. She stepped out by faith believing what he spoke would happen. She trusted in the Word of the Lord and lived.

When you feel you are in a hopeless situation trust in God. His word never fails. All that was required was for her to believe by faith and follow the instructions. God wants you to believe his word and follow his instructions. You shall not die but live.

Later on in the chapter we see that her son dies after getting sick. She had a hidden weight she was still carrying of sin that she had not forgiven herself of. She asked forgiveness of God but she held it in her heart. Out of the abundance of the heart the mouth speaketh. She blames the prophet for the death of her son saying he brought back her sin in remembrance to kill her son.

You may have suffered through many things and may have committed many sins but the Lord does not bring that back after he has forgiven you. If you have repented it is over. Let it go. He is not the God of dead issues but of life.

Watch what you say. There is power of life and death in the tongue. Do not speak death or accept it, believe the prophet and prosper.

Sometimes people have a tendency to not forgive themselves and allow that weight of guilt or shame on stay in their heart or mind. God forgives you when you truly repent and let it go, so let go of that weight. You gave it to the Lord and he cast it in the sea of forgetfulness. Stop playing reruns in your mind. God has promised life. It is the enemy who is playing on you to doubt God. Everyday this widow ate she remembered what she had said but never repented of it in her heart.

Don't blame others just because you are still holding onto it. She had spoken death and she remembered it but she did not cancel those words and speak life. The preacher is not preaching on you or throwing shade. The word of God has shined on the hidden thing. Ask God for forgiveness, and then forgive yourself. You may be rejecting your own self.

Don't allow death to come to your hopes and dreams because of your mouth. Cancel those negative and deadly words in Jesus name and speak life. This woman's son died. Her hope and dream died. She once hoped for him to live and grow up and take care of her in her old age. She may have dreamed of him marrying and having children continuing his father's lineage.

She opened her mouth and used the power of her tongue and spoke death. Be careful what you speak. Stop beating yourself with your own mouth. Stop speaking negative things and speak the word. God is not a man that he should lie and if he said it he will perform it.

The prophet asks for her dead son she is holding onto in her bosom. He takes her son that dead issue and lays a prophetic word on it. He lays himself on the boy three times and prays; In the name of the Father and of the Son and of the Holy Spirit symbolically. He speaks life and asks God for it for her son. God heard the prophet's prayers as he interceded for the life of the boy. The boy was restored to life.

The widow sacrificed all she had for another. She was chosen to bless and be blessed. She helped save the life of the prophet Elijah and he helped save the life of her son. She did not need a man for she had the word of the Lord there to remind her of how great God is and that he was her supply.

Stop grieving over what has passed on already. There is still life in your house and therefore there is still hope. You can kill hope and dreams with what you speak. Speak life and believe the word of the Lord that is given to you. You will prosper and live. You have been CHOSEN.

CHOSEN TO LIVE!

CHAPTER 10

Mary

Let us examine Mary the mother of Jesus. She was engaged to Joseph. They had not come together as husband and wife when she was found with child by the Holy Ghost.

The bible in Matt. 1:19-21 states:

> *"Then Joseph her husband, being a just man, and not willing to make her a public example, was minded to put her away privily.*
>
> *But while he thought on these things, behold, the angel of the Lord appeared unto him in a dream saying, Joseph, thou son of David, fear not to take unto thee Mary thy wife; for that which is conceived in her is of the Holy Ghost.*
>
> *And she shall bring forth a son, and thou shalt call his name JESUS: for he shall save his people from their sins."*

Joseph was a just man. He wanted to spare Mary the shame of open rejection. He wanted to do it in private. He planned not to take her as his wife because he could not understand how she was a virgin and now with child. He was to be the leader of the house but this child was not from him.

Mary was set to fulfill the prophecy given in Isaiah 7:14 which states:

> *"Therefore the Lord himself shall give you a sign; Behold, a virgin shall conceive, and bear a son, and shall call his name Immanuel."*

She was to fulfill the word of God while she was carrying the Word of God. Joseph obeys the instructions from the angel and marries Mary but does not consummate the marriage until after Jesus is born. When God puts a word in you it is not to be contaminated by the flesh.

In the book of Luke Chapter 1 the angel who was sent to Mary was Gabriel, a high ranking messenger angel.

Gabriel came and told Mary that:

- she was highly favored
- that the Lord was with her
- that she was blessed among women
- he also tells her not to fear
- and that she had found favor with God
- that she would conceive in her womb
- and bring forth a son and name him Jesus.

Mary sees the angel and was worried of what he meant. She was discerning and concerned because she could not understand how this could be since she was a virgin. The angel then breaks it down to her of how the Holy Ghost would come upon her and the power of God would overshadow her. She would birth a holy thing which shall be called the Son of God.

> *Luke 1:38:*
> *"And Mary said behold the handmaid of the Lord; be it unto me according to thy word. And the angel departed from her."*

Mary was to be married but then she was rejected. Joseph who had nothing to do with the conception wanted to put her away. Remember he was a just man. His thoughts even plagued him in his sleep until the angel came to minister unto him. He was told that Mary was chosen by God to birth the Word of God. A just man will accept the will of God, and so he did.

Jesus is the Word. God will not allow a man to contaminate his word before delivery. When God deposits a word in your womb it is by the power of the Holy Spirit that it is conceived. Like Mary you are to carry that word until the set time of its delivery. Man cannot shape that word, or claim that word that God gives you.

Mary was as a type of prophet who is given a word from God. The prophet of old prophesied it and the angel confirmed it. Mary then humbles herself as a servant of God to carry and then deliver that word so that others could be saved.

Many prophets have been quietly shut down by their leader because of the word they were given to deliver. The leader of the house decided that they were in error because they did not get the word from the leader himself.

Sometimes a leader may feel it is out of order if God did not come to them first. Prophet if God gave you a word he will confirm it and no man can change it. Stay submitted to the will of God. God have leaders who are just.

Mary had faith in God and was submitted, obedient, gave him praise and knew the word. She knew it was written in Isaiah that what the angel told her was true. It lined up with scripture. As a prophet you need to discern the word even if an angel delivers it to you. It should line up with what God has already spoken in his word and be confirmed.

In Christ there is neither male nor female and God does not have respect of person. Mary is a type of prophet whether male or female. Remember God is looking for a submitted, pure, and willing vessel to deposit his word.

Mary did not get upset knowing this could throw off her plans of marrying Joseph. She knew he might put her away. She knew she may be ostracized and shamed but, she remained faithful to God as his servant. God healed Joseph and his thinking by sending an angel to comfort him. Joseph accepted the will of God and loved his wife unconditionally. He could sleep with knowing that the will of God was to be accomplished in their lives. Joseph was a just man.

When you are pregnant with a word from God no one can tell you that you are not worthy to bring it forth. Mary accepted it by faith and humility as a servant. Never let man tell you that you are not worthy of the call of God. She had received a gift from the Holy Ghost and had to take care of it and trust God to bring it to fruition. She knew she had been chosen. Mary settled with the fact that she would submit and serve the Lord. She had been chosen to bring forth the Word of God. Prophet you have been CHOSEN!

CHOSEN TO BRING FORTH THE WORD OF GOD!

CHAPTER *11*

Woman Caught In Sin

John 8:2-5
"And early in the morning he came again into the temple,
and all the people came unto him; and he sat down and
taught them.

And the scribes and Pharisees brought unto him a woman
taken in adultery; and when they had set her in the midst,

They say unto him, Master, this woman was taken in
adultery, in the very act.

Now Moses in the law commanded us, that such should be
stoned: but what sayest thou?"

How was it that these religious Pharisees and scribes had nothing better to do early in the morning but go around looking to catch someone in sin? They had already purposed in their own mind what they would look for and who. They did not think to bring the man who was involved but only the woman.

It makes me think of how other religious folk today will try to judge some parts of the body of Christ and condemn them. They would love to separate them from the life that Jesus has to offer them. How often is the church accused of holding someone hostage to the sin committed as if there is no cure for sin?

Jesus has enough love and salvation for all. He desires that no one be lost so why are the most religious people always quick to expose and judge another and condemn them. They become graceless murderers thinking they are doing Jesus a favor. Where is the love and compassion that is to be had for all?

This woman was publically humiliated, her sin exposed, and dragged maybe half naked to Jesus. She was shamed before all who could see her early in the morning. There was no grace, love or mercy extended towards her when she needed it most. They were prepared to kill her physically. They had already murdered her in the spirit and she said nothing in her own defense.

This play out over and over in the churches today when a person falls from grace. They are not shown mercy or forgiveness. This is the time they need love and restoration. Because of this many leave the body of Christ going back into a world of sin and shame. The accused now becomes accuser of the brethren with a hardened heart.

This woman was caught in the act of adultery but that falls under the works of the flesh. She stands as a testament that regardless of the sin; if it is a work of the flesh it can be forgiven by Jesus.

> *Galatians 5:19-21*
> *"Now the works of the flesh are manifest, which are these; adultery, fornication, uncleanness, lasciviousness,*
>
> *Idolatry, witchcraft, hatred, variance, emulations, wrath, strife, seditions, heresies,*
>
> *Envying, murders, drunkenness, reveling, and such like: of the which I tell you before, as I have also told you in time past, that they which do such things shall not inherit the kingdom of God."*

They had no idea that they bought her to the right place and at the right time. Jesus is the only one who can pardon sin. This woman was helpless and did not offer excuse. She did not try to defend herself; she knew what was to follow. She realized that her life was in Jesus hands for the law had already condemned her. Man had already rejected her. She was at the mercy of the saviour and did not even know it.

Jesus did not look upon her but to the ground as he wrote. He did not eye her to cause one bit more of humiliation. Like a friend he handled her with care and compassion. He shared his love and mercy and pardons her of all her sin. She could start over in a new life without sin. She was given instructions to sin no more. If only those religious leaders could have been kind and caring like Jesus.

> *Galatians 6:1-2*
> *"Brethren, if a man be overtaken in a fault, ye which are spiritual, restore such a one in the spirit of meekness, considering thyself, lest thou also be tempted.*
>
> *Bear ye one another's burdens, and so fulfill the law of Christ.*

Christ took her burdens and he took my burdens and he continues to take on the burden of sin. It is up to you to choose to stand before him and accept his mercy and his salvation that he gives. Continue on in the newness of life following his instructions and sin no more.

She was chosen to receive salvation. Christ died for the world. We have all been chosen to receive this same grace and mercy extended to us. We have all been chosen to be saved, but everyone does not respond to Christ's invitation the same.

Romans 8:33-34:
"Who shall lay anything to the charge of God's elect? It is God that justifieth.

Who is he that condemneth? It is Christ that died, yea rather, that is risen again, who is even at the right hand of God, who also maketh intercession for us."

Just as Jesus stood between life and death for this woman and made intercession for her life, he still intercedes today for us before God. No man can condemn another for their sin. Jesus blood was shed for all.

These religious leaders had respect of persons because they did not bring the man forth that was caught in sin as well. They plotted against Jesus and this woman. With that said, they themselves broke the law.

Deuteronomy 17:5-6
"Then shalt thou bring forth that man or that woman, which have committed that wicked thing, unto thy gates, even that man or that woman, and shalt stone them with stones, till they die.

At the mouth of two witnesses, or three witnesses shall he that is worthy of death be put to death; but at the mouth of one witness he shall not be put to death."

There were many witnesses against this woman. They were eager to stone her to death but there was one witness that was greater than them all. Jesus Christ was the only one who could forgive sin. He was the advocate on her behalf and when he asked where her accusers were, she correctly replied no man Lord.

She accepted Christ as her Lord and savior. He delivered her from sin and its shame and penalty of death. When others are trying to destroy you and reject you, know that you have a friend who is there for you. Jesus will not condemn you as long as you follow him.

> *James 2:9-10*
> *"But if ye have respect to persons, ye commit sin, and are convinced of the law as transgressors.*
>
> *For whosoever shall keep the whole law, and yet offend in one point, he is guilty of all."*

Jesus came for the poor in spirt, the despised, the rejected, and the weak. He came to give wisdom, peace, life, wholeness and acceptance. Most of all he came in love to show love and to share love. This woman was restored and made whole for she had been chosen because of his love.

CHOSEN TO BE SAVED!

CHAPTER 12

The Man At The Pool

Jesus is on his way to a feast of the Jews in Jerusalem and on his way he notice at the pool of Bethesda a great multitude of people. These people are waiting for the traditional moving of the water. There was a certain time that an angel would come down and the water would be troubled and the first one in would be healed of their affliction. Jesus the well of water was troubled this day.

Jesus notices a man that had been at this pool for thirty and eight years. He knew that he had been there a long time and so He says unto him, "wilt thou be made whole?"

No matter what your struggle is Jesus has taken notice. It may seem like a long time but your answer is right there. This man wanted to be made whole but he thought he had to wait for the help of man.

> *John 5:7*
> *"The impotent man answered him, Sir, I have no man, when the water is troubled, to put me into the pool: but while I am coming, another steppeth down before me."*

This man was impotent meaning he had no physical strength. He was weak and helpless. Can you see this man when the water is troubled trying to crawl or pull himself over the side of the pool; trying so hard through the work of the flesh to get in and being too late every time?
Do you know how he must have felt to feel the wind of a person stepping past him and watching them getting healed splashing around in the pool?

Thirty eight years he waited for a man to help him reach his potential. He was stuck looking at that pool. He could not see any other way and his faith was stuck in tradition. He was left alone and could not help himself. His sight was limited at an earthly level. He hoped that flesh would help him. He yet felt alone and rejected.

This man needed to hear a new sound. There were many voices around this pool. Jesus does not call a name but the man is no longer looking at the pool but his focus is now on Jesus. Jesus just asks a simple question. The man's faith is stirred and he began to hope this man he called "Sir" could help.

He had put his faith in Jesus blindly not even realizing who he was. His mustard seed faith was activated when his thoughts changed, his heart changed, and his focus changed.

This man for thirty and eight years was poor, reduced to begging to survive. He could not marry, work, or have children. He received a word from the Lord and his life changed. Thirty is symbolic of the right time for ministry and eight symbolizes a new beginning. This man had been chosen and he was about to get a new lease on life.

Jesus had compassion and he stop where he saw a need. He tells the man to rise, take up his bed and walk. The man was made whole and rose and took up that thing he was bound to for so many years and walked. Walking symbolized that he progressed in life.

It is mentioned that it was on the Sabbath when Jesus performed a miracle. No work was to be done on the Sabbath and Jesus had broken tradition. The man was healed after he also broke tradition. He looked to the new Way. He did not have to wait for an angel because the Healer was personally there with him.

You do not have to feel bound to tradition. You do not need man to get you to a place of productivity. Jesus is standing there in your situation no matter how long you have been there and no matter how hard the battle has been. Jesus can break any bondage that is holding you back from living life in its fullness.

Like this man you have to change your focus and look towards Jesus. You need to see and hear the Word of God. Once you develop a personal relationship with him talking to you, and you talking to him, things will begin to happen.

This weak man grew stronger as he became obedient to the Word. Jesus is the word of God. He could see things from Jesus point of view. He was able to look up and his thoughts were now higher. He was able to come up to another level seeing things from a heavenly perspective.

Do not give up. Keep faith in Jesus. The bible says vain is the help of man, so trust Jesus. You are not forgotten. Jesus knew before he talked to the man that he had been that way for a long time. Jesus knows and is with you through the process. He is waiting on you to respond.

You are not alone. It is time to change your thought pattern and focus on the will of God for your life. With Jesus you can rise, walk, and be in control of that thing that is holding you down. Take it with you as a testimony to help someone else. You have been chosen to rise above your circumstance.

CHOSEN TO BREAK TRADITION!

CHAPTER 13

Stephen

Stephen was one of seven men chosen to help take care of the widows who were being neglected. He handled benevolences and also became a very powerful preacher. It is stated that Stephen was:

- of honest report
- full of the Holy Ghost
- full of wisdom
- full of faith
- full of power
- and did great wonders and miracles

Being full of the Holy Ghost he was also full of power. You can only expect that he would move in miracles. His faith was full, he never ran low on it. He was honest and wise. Stephen was a preacher of the word of God in excellence.

Truth will always expose a lie. There were certain people of the synagogue of the Libertines, some elders and scribes who would argue with Stephen over the truth that he shared. They could not resist the wisdom or the Spirit by which he spoke and resorted to silence him by murder. He was excellent in wisdom and expounding of the scriptures.

These men who disputed with Stephen resorted to encouraging false witnesses to call Stephen blasphemous against the laws of Moses and against the temple. They stirred the people to capture him and put him on trial.

Stephen defends himself with the scripture stating how the Jews themselves had broken the laws of Moses and dishonored the temple in times past. During the time of the trial, it is written that he sat with his face shining like an angel. Stephen was being rejected but he was not forsaken. Having been weak in their argument and convicted in their hearts the Jewish council decides to stone him to death. Stephen was the first martyr of the Christian church.

He continued in the love of God and truth until his death. Even as he was being stoned to death he looked to heaven and was able to see Christ stand to receive him home. Dying he forgave them for his murder and prayed for them.

There are going to be many who will think that what you are presenting is heretical and try to dispel the teachings of the Word of God. The Libertines were a Jewish sect of freed men and their descendants who were released from Roman slavery and built a synagogue. They held very strictly to the laws of Moses and the temple and any talk by the Christians were seen as blasphemous.

The truth of the word of God will prevail over error. As a minister of the gospel you need to be prepared to be able to defend what you believe. There are even other denominations within Christendom which will reject you as one in error when you bring the truth of God's word. Stephen knew the scriptures from Genesis to the time of Christ. He studied the word of God.

When others cannot refute the word they will resort to lying on you and trying to destroy you. They are ultimately rejecting Christ and trying to silence you. Stephen was unmovable and had an inner peace keeping his eyes on Christ up until he died. Do not let anyone distort your vision. Keep the faith and finish to obtain the prize like Stephen whose name meant wreath or crown.

Bloody clothes were thrown at the feet of Saul whose name later was changed to Paul. Stephen's death bought conviction to the heart of Saul which led to him receiving salvation and writing much of the New Testament.

Stand on the solid rock and waver not. God is sitting high and looking at you below. He sees your struggles and he sees your persistence. When you teach the word of God there will be some who will not receive. They are not rejecting you but rejecting the truth you bring. They cannot do anything against the truth but they may retaliate against you

Pray for them when they say all manner of evil against you and try to damage you with lies. The truth will cut them to the heart and bring conviction. They may lash out at you personally but they are really persecuting Christ in you. Forgive them and keep the light shining. Be that witness for the Lord and live the life of Christlikeness so much so that others are changed. Die out to your flesh and live a life pleasing to him.

Look to Jesus knowing that he has not forsaken you. He is there even in your persecutions until your last breath. He will strengthen you to remain faithful to the end. Be like Christ, forgiving and praying for those who reject, hurt, and try to murder you for your belief. Pray and see them from a heavenly perspective.

Stay faithful to truth being a witness of the love of Christ even until death. You will see the glory of God, the risen saviour and be crowned with everlasting life. You have been Chosen.

CHOSEN TO BE A WITNESS!

CHAPTER 14
Paul

Saul of Tarsus was the original title of the Apostle Paul before his conversion. He was a known persecutor of the early Christian church. He was devoted to what he believed as truth and saw the early Christians as heretics worthy of death. He felt his mission was to remove all Christians from the face of the earth and destroy the church.

Paul before his conversion was over zealous and lifted in pride. He was a Pharisee and a member of the Sanhedrin and a teacher. Paul had a group who followed him to search out the Christians, killing and scattering them.

In causing the Christians to scatter, he unknowingly pushed them to go abroad and preach the gospel. Even this havoc worked for the some good. Saul gave the consent to the stoning of Stephen and bloody clothes were laid at his feet.

Acts 9:3-9
"And as he journeyed, he came near Damascus: and suddenly there shined round about him a light from heaven.

And he fell to the earth, and heard a voice saying unto him. Saul, Saul, why persecutest thou me?

And he said, who art thou, Lord? And the Lord said, I am Jesus whom thou persecutest; it is hard for thee to kick against the pricks.

And he trembling and astonished said, Lord, what wilt thou have me to do? And the Lord said unto him, Arise, and go into the city, and it shall be told thee what thou must do.

And the men which journeyed with him stood speechless, hearing a voice, but seeing no man.

And Saul arose from the earth; and when his eyes were opened, he saw no man: but they led him by the hand, and brought him into Damascus.

And he was there three days without sight, and neither did eat or drink."

Paul thought he was doing the right thing in defending what he had been taught in the laws of Moses. He believed that the Christians were a heretical group, but now he will come face to face with the Truth.

He had no idea of the change that would take place in his life. As he was on his way to slaughter more Christians; he has a divine encounter with Jesus. A light from heaven is shining all around and he falls off his horse to the ground. He was sitting high but is bought low and he is to the ground. Flesh must be bought low and come into submission to the will of God.

The first time Paul says Lord, he had a true desire to know who was speaking to him. You have to know Christ before you can receive him. The second time Paul says Lord, he says it out of humble submission to the voice of the Lord. Paul had been chosen to be converted.

After coming to know the Lord through the intimacy of communication and prayer he knew his voice. He felt the power of his presence. He saw the glory of the Lord. Paul continued to get an understanding of what Jesus desired of him. He was able to discern the voice of the Lord as a sheep and follow him. Paul was careful of how he heard and was still and listened as Jesus spoke to him.

Paul waited for a response from the Lord after asking him questions. Jesus reveals himself to Paul. When you get to the place like Paul to fall down and submit yourself to Christ he will reveal himself to you. You will be enlightened with revelation knowledge of the Truth of God's Word.

You have to work out your own soul salvation as Paul did with reverential fear and trembling. Paul is given distinct instructions of what was required of him. In obedience and blind faith he ventures into what the Lord has told him to do. He gets up and moves forward in a new way.

When God has given you instructions, he will send all the help you need to accomplish the task. Paul could not see but the men that were with him they heard the voice of the Lord and like Paul could see no man. The men never bowed down in submission to the voice, though they remained submitted to Paul.

Paul had been blinded naturally but the men were not; they were still blind spiritually. Paul had insight into the will of God for his life but the men with him did not. God used them to help Paul begin his journey towards his destiny.

Paul had been chosen to see things differently. He no longer looked down on others but begin to look up to Jesus. He went where the Lord sent him and not where he wanted to go.

When he arrived at Ananias house and he fasted for three days Ananias laid hands on him and the scales fell from his eyes. Paul received his sight again and was filled with the Holy Ghost and baptized. Then he eats meat and was strengthened. Following this he preached Christ in the synagogues.

If you want to understand the purpose God has for you, it is good to fast. It is good to deny the flesh so that your spirit man can hear clearly and be strengthened. Paul was able to preach to both Jew and Gentile. He was chosen to change and then change the world.

Following Paul through his missionary journeys you will see how he was rejected first because of fear from believers and then from those who also rejected the Christian doctrines and Christ. Paul faced many hardships and trials.

Paul worked long and hard and suffered much being beaten, imprisoned, scourged, stoned, shipwrecked, hungry and thirsty, homeless, cold and naked reviled and persecuted, deserted and threatened with death. He was mistreated and verbally abused and had many sleepless nights. He was now the one being persecuted and he eventually was beheaded and martyred.

Jesus suffered rejection and the apostles suffered rejection. To reign with Christ you will suffer. God is with you even to the end. Jesus loved Paul and he personally offered salvation to him. He was chosen to receive the Lord as his saviour and accept the new life he had to offer him.

Man may not understand why you do what you do. They may not accept the new and improved you when you follow the Lord. That is okay. God want to heal you, bless you, love you, strengthen you and send you out as a witness of his love.

When those who stood with you no longer do, pray for them. Love them to life. Believe God that they will also see the light and allow God to renew their minds and hearts. Paul was called as an apostle and separated unto the gospel of God Paul had been renewed in Christ and was a builder of the New Testament church having written 14 of the 27 books. Paul was chosen and you the reader have also been chosen by God to change.

CHOSEN TO BE CHANGED!

CHAPTER 15

Jesus

Finally let us look at Jesus. He was the only begotten of the Father, the Messiah. Jesus the son of David was chosen to save mankind. Jesus is the saviour of the world. He was rarely called saviour in the scriptures.

This Jesus was born of a woman and had a call on his life that was to be fulfilled. The anointed one so rejected by men. This is Jesus, God incarnate, who we call Emmanuel which means God with us. When he came he was rejected by the world yet he sacrificed himself for it.

Jesus was about his father's business and was publically announced by God. He was baptized and filled with the Holy Spirit. His own family and friends were skeptical of him. They could not see past him being just the carpenter's son.

Yes, this Jesus set himself aside for the work of the Father. He was led into the wilderness for forty days on a supernatural fast. He was tempted by Satan and had dominion over him.

Jesus who was different; he taught different not like the Pharisees. Even the priests rejected him. Yet Jesus performed many miracles, cast out many devils, healed the sick and raised the dead.

Our Jesus was imprisoned, spit on, beaten all night long and mocked. His own disciples deserted him and he was crucified and died.

He endured and suffered because of his LOVE for us. He was chosen to make a way for mankind to get back in right standing with God. He laid down his life and became The Way closing the gap that separated us from the Father.

Matthew 27:46
"And about the ninth hour Jesus cried with a loud voice, saying Eli, Eli, lama sabachthani? That is to say My God, My God, why hast thou forsaken me?"

Can you imagine how he felt? Jesus suffered a rejection we can never really imagine. His integrity remained intact. His love was still onboard for others. He kept forgiveness as his right hand man. He did not show off and try to prove himself to others of who he was. He let his actions speak for him. He was rejected by man but chosen by God.

Jesus ran his race and finished his course, and when he finished it, all sin was done away with. Death was abolished. He had taught and served with humility, then became a sacrifice for all our sin. The purpose of his life was finished all alone at the cross. Yet that was not the end. He arose in three days with all power.

Rejection does not end your purpose or story! It is written, "Greater love hath no man than this that a man would lay down his life for his friends." We were in sin and he called us friends if we do what he commands us to do.

There must be a response to the call to salvation. You become his chosen when you accept by faith who he is and what he has done for you and repent. Then follow him. You continue to respond by keeping his commandments. He showed you love chose you out of his love, and command that you too, love.

Even the one who had sold him out and betrayed him; he was called and chosen as a disciple and an apostle until in his heart he rejected Christ. When you stop doing as he commands you are then in disobedience. His love is still available to you and waiting for you to come back repentant and continue the course that he set for you before it is too late.

In John 15:17-21 Jesus says,

> "These things I command you, that ye love one another.
>
> If the world hate you, ye know that it hated me before it hated you.
>
> If ye were of the world, the world would love his own, but I HAVE CHOSEN YOU out of the world, therefore the world hateth you.
>
> Remember the word that I said unto you. The servant is not greater than his lord. If they have persecuted me, they will also persecute you; if they have kept my sayings, they will keep yours also.
>
> But all these things they will do unto you for my name's sake, because they know not him that sent me."

God knew before the world was formed who would accept him and who would reject him. Remember when you feel like you are being rejected that they are not rejecting you, but Christ in you. It is a blessing to be chosen by God.

> Psalm 65:4
> "Blessed is the man whom thou choosest, and causeth to approach unto thee, that he may dwell in thy courts; we

shall be satisfied with the goodness of thy house, even of thy
holy temple."

Jesus Christ suffered so much rejection then how much more shall we? The servant is not greater than his master. Even when your closest friends scatter press on and continue the work you was chosen to do. You have power to continue; the power of love and the power of forgiveness.

II Timothy 1:8-9 tells us:

> *"Be not thou therefore ashamed of the testimony of our*
> *Lord, nor of me his prisoner; but be thou partaker of the*
> *afflictions of the gospel according to the power of God.*
>
> *Who hath saved us, and called us with an holy calling, not*
> *according to our works, but according to his own purpose*
> *and grace, which was given us in Christ Jesus before the*
> *world began."*

You are going to go through some things and God knew it before the world began. He is there in eternity and saw your afflictions on his timeline. He had designed you for purpose that has to be fulfilled. Do not give up. Do not turn and walk away. God knew you would be faithful, and he chose you.

He knew that you would bring forth fruit and it would remain. Don't fret over what others do, just know you are working out the plan of God for your life.

> *In John 15:16 Jesus says:*
> *"Ye have not chosen me, but I have chosen you, and*
> *ordained you, that you should go and bring forth fruit,*

and that your fruit should remain: that whatsoever ye shall ask of the Father in my name, he may give it you."

Jesus was rejected and despised and yet was chosen by God to bring salvation to man. He made a response and completed his purpose. God has chosen you and he needs a response from you. Will you complete the task he has called you to? Will you continue on despite the rejection? Can you love your enemy without prejudice? Can you lay down your life for another?

God has chosen you and given you the weapons of love and forgiveness to use to keep you going forward. It is up to you to follow his commandments. If you choose not to keep his commandments is there a penalty for that? Yes there is. There is consequences when you turn away to man or to sin for acceptance instead of his Beloved.

In Isaiah 65:11-16 it states:

> *But ye are they that forsake my holy mountain, that prepare a table for that troop, and that furnish the drink offering unto that number*

> *Therefore will I number you to the sword, and ye shall all bow down to the slaughter: because when I called, ye did not answer; when I spake, ye did not hear; but did evil before mine eyes, and did choose that wherein I delighted not.*

> *Therefore thus saith the Lord my servants shall eat; but ye shall be hungry; behold my servants shall drink; but*

ye shall be thirsty; behold my servants shall rejoice, but ye shall be ashamed:

Behold my servants shall sing for joy of heart, but ye shall cry for sorrow of heart, and shall howl for vexation of spirit.

And ye shall leave your name for a curse unto my chosen: for the Lord God shall slay thee, and call his servants by another name:

That he that blesseth himself in the earth shall bless himself in the God of truth; and he that sweareth in the earth shall swear by the God of Truth; because the former troubles are forgotten, and because they are hid from mine eyes."

Matthew 25:47
"And that servant, which knew his lord's will, and prepared not himself, neither did according to his will, shall be beaten with many stripes."

Finally and most dreaded and hope for Romans 6:23 it states,

"For the wages of sin is death; but the gift of God is eternal life through Jesus Christ our Lord."

God chose you and he gave you power to choose him. Choose the gift he has given to you. He will not make you follow and do. He waits for a response from you. Adversities of life may come and often they are the stripes for disobedience. You do not want to be as they say caught with your work undone.

How does that happen? If you die before you accept salvation your work is undone and you will be paid the wages for sin. If you remain you will miss the rapture of the saints and will go through tribulation being sorely persecuted. It will also be hard because the Holy Spirit will be taken out with the saints as well.

In Jeremiah 7:13-15 it is written:

> *"And now, because ye have done all these works, saith the Lord, and I spake unto you, rising up early and speaking, but ye heard not; and I called you, but ye answered not;*
>
> *Therefore will I do unto this house, which is called by my name, wherein ye trust and unto the place which I gave to you and to your fathers, as I have done in Shiloh.*
>
> *And I will cast you out of my sight, as I have cast out all your brethren, even the whole seed of Ephraim."*

There is a price to be paid; God will remove you from his sight. When you choose not to follow his law you choose to be captive to sin. You choose to not know him. You lack bread which is the word of God who is Jesus Christ, and you lack the water which is the Holy Spirit. You will die without both. You die naturally and spiritually without bread or water. Jesus is the way out of death and destruction.

> *Isaiah 5:13-16*
> *"Therefore my people are gone into captivity, because they have no knowledge: and their honorable men are famished, and their multitude dried up with thirst.*
>
> *Therefore hell hath enlarged herself, and opened her mouth without measure: and their glory, and their multitude, and their pomp, and he that rejoiceth, shall descend into it.*

And the mean man shall be bought down, and the mighty man shall be humbled, and the eyes of the lofty shall be humbled.

But the Lord of hosts shall be exalted in judgment, and God that is holy shall be sanctified in righteousness."

In closing as you have read, you have been chosen. You have been chosen to salvation and to work. God is love and sent his love and all you need to do is receive love and share it. You are unique and God designed you that way.

There is something for us all to do and there will always be naysayers and persecution. You must know that you have been fearfully and wonderfully made and marvelous is the work of the Lord. God does not care whether you are male or female; all have been chosen to salvation.

Jesus is the healer of all hurt. He has been there. In Psalms 147 it is written that he heals the broken in heart and binds up their wounds. How does he do it? He does it with love. Love is the key to overcoming the hurt of rejection. Once you apply this balm of Gilead, wrap it in forgiveness.

Do not retaliate, fear, or run. You have more power than you realize. You are not just a winner but you are an overcomer through Christ Jesus and accepted in the beloved. You may be rejected by man but you have been chosen by God.

YOU HAVE BEEN CHOSEN AND GOD LOVES YOU!

Revelation 17:14
"These shall make war with the lamb, and the Lamb shall overcome them: for he is Lord of lords, and King of kings: and they that are with him are Called, and CHOSEN, and FAITHFUL."

AMEN

CPSIA information can be obtained
at www.ICGtesting.com
Printed in the USA
BVHW031428071119
563198BV00002B/12/P

9 781796 069006